DEVELOPMENT WITHOUT DAMAGE

Not for People

rol Inskipp

Evans

Contents

Introduction

It is easy to take nature for granted because it exists all around us – in parks and woods, at the beach, in the mountains and oceans. Over the past two centuries, however, wilderness areas around the world have been in decline, and important ecosystems such as rainforests are being destroyed by human activity. Today, governments, organisations and individuals are beginning to appreciate the value of these areas, and are increasingly looking for ways of preserving them for future generations.

Trekkers in the Italian Alps. As people began to enjoy leisure activities such as hiking, they also started to appreciate the value of protecting wilderness areas from human development.

The World's Wild Places

For much of human history most land on Earth was wilderness, unaffected by human activity. This wild area was thought of as a place to fear and avoid – even somewhere inhabited by monsters. During the nineteenth century views changed, and people began to appreciate wilderness areas for their own sake. Previously people had explored wild places to increase their knowledge of the world. Now they walked in the wilderness, climbed mountains and rafted rivers for pleasure as well.

The Conservation Movement

By the second half of the nineteenth century, wild places were disappearing in many parts of the world, particularly in more economically developed countries (MEDCs). Population increases meant more space was needed for housing, and industrialisation resulted in the growth of cities. This loss of wilderness areas led to the start of the conservation movement, intended to protect and preserve the natural landscape. Beginning in the United States, but quickly spreading to the United Kingdom, mainland Europe and Australia, preservation orders were placed on species that were thought to be under threat, and whole areas were set aside to be protected by law from human encroachment.

Human Impact on the Natural World

In the late twentieth century it became clear that just putting aside areas of land and declaring them 'wilderness' or 'protected' was not enough. All natural environments are connected in some way and what happens outside national parks affects what happens inside them. Air pollution from towns and cities causes poor air quality in some national parks. Climate change has an impact on all parts of the world, including national parks that were once considered safe from human interference. Now it is widely understood that to look after the world's remaining wild places we need to protect the natural environment as a whole, including resources such as air and water.

As more and more people live in urban areas and have busier lives, many find that in their leisure time they have a greater need to experience the natural world. Here they can find open spaces, fresh air and relaxation. This revived appreciation of the natural world has resulted in plans to protect nature in a sustainable way.

EXPERT VIEW

'When we contemplate the whole globe as one great dewdrop, striped and dotted with continents and islands, flying through space with the other stars, all singing and shining together as one, the whole universe appears as an infinite storm of beauty.'

JOHN MUIR, FOUNDER OF THE NATIONAL PARK MOVEMENT IN THE UNITED STATES

CASE STUDY

North America: The National Park Movement

The conservation movement began in the United States in the 1860s, when preservation orders were placed on the Yosemite Valley and areas where trees such as the sequoia (the tallest in the world) grew. In 1872 Yellowstone became the world's first national park. Other countries soon established their own national parks, including Banff National Park in Canada in 1885. Efforts to preserve and protect North America's wilderness areas have continued since then, and in recent years several new programmes have been initiated. These include efforts to preserve the valuable ecosystems of the Great Lakes, the Great Bear Rainforest in Canada (see page 41) and others.

The Yellowstone River winds its way through Yellowstone National Park – the first national park to be established.

Nature and Tourism

Over the last 20 years, people in industrialised countries around the world have had more money to spend and more free time. This has led to an enormous growth in the leisure and tourism industries. Scenic landscapes and natural environments such as forests and wetlands are popular attractions. However, this rise in tourism has had a detrimental effect on nature.

The Effects of Nature Tourism

In some less economically developed countries (LEDCs) such as Laos, Vietnam and South Africa, the growth of tourism is rising faster than it is in MEDCs. These countries are rich in wildlife and a large part of their foreign tourism is linked to nature activities.

Nature tourism is increasing at around 10–12 per cent every year. Most of tourism's expansion is occurring in and around the world's natural areas. In places such as the Galapagos islands, the Seychelles and Kenya, wildlife watching is the main basis for tourism.

Tourism has grown so fast that it has led to damaging environmental impacts, such as poorly planned tourism developments, pollution, and loss of wildlife and natural resources like forests and wetlands. In many places tourism is actually

Safaris like this one in Kenya are an important source of income for many African countries.

In countries like Vietnam, local guides take groups of tourists on treks. Many of these guides were once wildlife hunters but now they earn an income from tourism instead.

destroying the very thing that tourists have come to see. Tourism can also place economic pressure on local people, especially the very poor.

Controlling Nature Tourism

Communities require training and support to develop the skills needed for employment in the tourism industry or to set up their own tourism businesses. Systems are also needed to make sure that the income from tourism is shared fairly among groups of communities. A community that lives close to the entrance of a national park, for example, will have far better opportunities to benefit from tourism than a community in a more remote area that tourists rarely visit.

With careful management tourism can benefit all – wildlife, environments, tourists, hosts and host countries – without harming the environmental resources on which it depends. If managed well, tourism can be a powerful positive force for conservation. It can also provide additional income for local communities and revenue for governments, which are especially valuable in LEDCs.

EXPERT VIEW

'If you put more and more hotels along the beaches then of course that is going to have an environmental impact. Eventually there will come a time when the quality of beaches will have become so poor that people will not want to come here because the product you are offering has lost its value.'
ENVIRONMENTAL CONSULTANT, MAURITIUS

FACTS IN FOCUS
Tourism Economics

Tourism is the largest business in the world economy and is responsible for over 10 per cent of gross domestic product (GDP) worldwide. International tourism receipts totalled £1,000 million a day in 2006. Tourism is one of the main sources of money earned by 83 per cent of LEDCs and the leading export for 33 per cent of the poorest countries. For the world's 40 poorest countries, tourism is the second most important source of foreign exchange after oil.

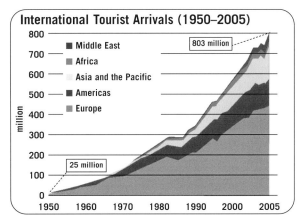

International Tourist Arrivals (1950–2005)

- Middle East
- Africa
- Asia and the Pacific
- Americas
- Europe

803 million

25 million

Source: World Tourism Organization

The total increase in tourist arrivals worldwide shown here is broken down by region. Europe has seen the biggest increase and Africa the smallest increase.

Kapawi in Ecuador is a lodge that works with the indigenous people to provide a tourist destination that minimises the environmental impact of tourism.

Sustainable Tourism

Tourism can play an important role in conserving natural environments. It can provide a source of income for people living in areas that are rich in plants and animals and have attractive natural environments. In many areas, however, poor management and growing numbers of tourists have led to pollution and the destruction of important habitats. Animals have often migrated away from tourist areas and sometimes even local people have been forced out.

To overcome these problems, members of the tourist industry are working to meet the needs of tourists and host regions, while at the same time protecting and improving opportunities for the future. This is the meaning of sustainable tourism.

Obstacles to Sustainable Tourism

Some tourism operators believe that not enough people demand holidays that improve the environment and community welfare of the places they visit. They say that until this happens little will improve. Operators often continue to sell the holidays they have sold in the past because sustainable holidays cost more. Most operators do not educate tourists about the importance of having a sustainable holiday.

Many operators prefer to sell package holidays. These combine flight, transport from the destination airport and holiday accommodation. Package holidays offer value for money and the opportunity to relax in a safe environment, which is what many people want. While package holidays are very

TAKE ACTION

By making informed choices before and during a trip we can all help to make our holidays more sustainable. With a little planning it is possible to improve the quality of a trip, while making a real difference to the people and places we visit.

popular with large numbers of tourists, many of them damage environments and are unsustainable.

The Role of Tour Operators

Tour operators have a major role to play in making holidays more sustainable. They can influence the development of destinations and control the numbers of tourists visiting them. Decisions made by operators also affect the behaviour of their customers and the well-being of local communities.

Tourism operators face the challenge of ensuring the industry is sustainable and maintaining the benefits from tourism at the same time. Most operators recognise that a clean and safe environment is vital to their success. However, not many of them have the management experience to organise tours that limit the negative effects on the environment. To overcome this problem, several tour operators from different parts of the world have joined forces to create the Tour Operators' Initiative for Sustainable Tourism. Members are working together with the United Nations and World Tourism Organisation to develop ideas and projects in sustainable tourism.

CASE STUDY

Turkey: Sustainable Tourism at Cirali

Cirali, a coastal community in south-west Turkey, has created a successful model of sustainable tourism with the help of the Worldwide Fund for Nature (WWF). The region is one of the most important for nature in the Mediterranean, but it is also among the most affected by mass tourism development. Cirali Beach is one of the major nesting sites for the endangered loggerhead turtle. With the help of locals, kiosks and restaurants built too close to the shore have been moved further from the coast. The WWF has also designed an environmentally friendly land-use plan. Tourism activities have been initiated, providing income for the community as well as creating support for conservation. Many of the young people of Cirali have trained to become nature guides. Several activities are in place to protect the loggerhead turtles, and their numbers are now increasing.

Cirali Beach in Turkey has become a good example of sustainable tourism practices thanks to initiatives by the WWF and local people.

Ecotourism

Ecotourism is responsible travel to natural areas that conserves the environment and improves the well-being of local people. Ecotourism aims to build the awareness and respect of tourists for the environment and culture of the place they are visiting. Local people and conservation projects usually benefit financially from ecotourism.

The Value of Ecotourism

Ecotourism can encourage communities to conserve the local environment and wildlife. In Guyana, for example, the rainforest is now being conserved for tourism purposes rather than being cut down for short-term financial gain.

The Napo Wildlife Center in Ecuador protects local culture and biodiversity. It is a joint venture with the community and 90 per cent of employees are local. Untouched rainforest covering 210 sq km is protected by the centre, working closely with Yasuni National Park. As the area is so large, sustainable populations of even large predators like jaguars are maintained in the rainforest. The Napo Center has encouraged the organisation of all the communities that live in the park into one unit that helps to protect the area in the long term.

One of the most diverse ecosystems in Africa lies in Kakum National Park in Ghana. The national park is highly threatened and tourism is being developed to create funds to help conserve the park. A walkway has been constructed through the treetops to give visitors a unique way of experiencing the rainforest. The canopy walkway and a new visitor centre have increased visitors to the area, 80 per cent of whom are Ghanaian. Park entrance fees have contributed significantly to the conservation of the park. The local economy has also benefited, as local people sell handicrafts, food and lodging to tourists.

Greenwashing and Certification

The word ecotourism can be misused, however. Some companies exploit the eco-label to

FACTS IN FOCUS
Economic Benefits of Ecotourism

A total of 80 per cent of the cost of all-inclusive package tours goes to airlines, hotels and other international companies. In contrast, eco-lodges hire and purchase locally, and sometimes put as much as 95 per cent of the cost into the local economy.

encourage tourists to sign up for their holidays. This is known as 'greenwashing'.

So how do we find a true ecotourism holiday? Although there is no international scheme, there are regional or country schemes that certify ecotourism holidays in many parts of the world. The Eco Certification Program has been developed

The rainforest walkway in Ghana has contributed to an improvement in the local economy, attracting tourists and encouraging locals to conserve their environment.

by the tourist industry in Australia. Under this initiative, nature tour businesses are looked at carefully to find out if they are achieving real ecotourism goals. Certification provides an assurance that is valuable to everyone involved – those working in the tourist industry, protected-area managers, local communities and travellers. Similar schemes include the Certification Network of the Americas, the Blue Flag and Protected Area Network in Europe, and Sustainable Tourism in Costa Rica.

EXPERT VIEW

'The future of Kenya tourism is green. The trend in Kenya is to create a tourism industry which will be low impact. It will meet our needs without compromising the ability of future generations to meet their needs. Those who realise this, and begin to change their thinking and actions, will reap the long-term benefits.'
JUDY GONA, EXECUTIVE DIRECTOR, ECOTOURISM SOCIETY OF KENYA

The Komodo National Park in Indonesia helps conserve the rare Komodo dragon and many other species. It is developing an ecotourism programme in association with the Nature Conservancy.

Responsible Tourism

Although many schemes are improving the way that tourism affects nature, few of these take into account the environmental effects of air travel. Aeroplanes release large amounts of carbon dioxide into the atmosphere and contribute to climate change (see page 36). There are now a number of low-cost airlines, which means that more people can afford to travel by air to their holiday destinations. The income generated by increased numbers of tourists is important, especially in LEDCs, but many people are concerned about the environmental impacts.

Which is more important – benefiting communities in less developed countries, or reducing the effect on the environment?

Increasingly, there are ways to do both. Some people now choose to travel on holiday by boat or by train instead of by aeroplane. In countries including the United Kingdom and the United States, special schemes have been introduced that allow people travelling by air to 'offset' their effect on climate change. These schemes include paying a small amount of money for trees to be planted or contributing to renewable-energy projects. Such solutions make tourism more responsible.

TAKE ACTION

If you are going on an organised holiday, ask your tour operator for their responsible tourism policy. Check the environmental policy of your accommodation, too.

Responsible holidays can include hiking in the rainforest, cycling in your home country or even taking a cruise in Antarctica.

CASE STUDY

Gambia: Responsible Tourism Policies

Some countries have adopted responsible tourism policies. In Gambia, for example, where tourism is important to the economy, the government is attempting to change the country's image as a cheap winter-sun destination dominated by mass tourism. Where once the beaches were filled with local people approaching tourists to sell goods, stalls have now been set up. Tourists are less intimidated, and income for the beach vendors has doubled. Codes of practice and training programmes have been introduced for taxi drivers, official tourist guides and market sellers so that they understand the needs and expectations of tourists. It is hoped that tourists will enjoy their holidays more by having meaningful interactions with local people.

A local market in Gambia. Responsible tourism policies aim to improve the livelihoods of local communities.

Planning a Responsible Holiday

Individuals play an important role in responsible tourism. When choosing a holiday, people can consider the destination, accommodation, any travel involved and their choice of tour operator. The secret to having a responsible trip is to be well informed. Operators can be found online that specialise in responsible tourism. There are numerous guidebooks with information on environmental issues and the cultural traditions of tourist destinations. By making concerns known about the environmental policies of tour operators and hotels, individuals can encourage them to provide responsible holidays. Asking simple questions, such as whether or not operators support projects that benefit local communities or whether they employ local people, can raise awareness of the need for responsible tourism.

Wildlife Watching

Wildlife watching has become a popular leisure activity. This can be as simple as bird watching in a local area, or going on a specialist holiday such as a safari. Wildlife trips, such as whale and dolphin spotting, are frequently on offer on package holidays. Visitors may take a wildlife trip just for entertainment, but they will learn about the animals they have seen and are likely to return home with a stronger commitment to conservation.

Risks to Wildlife

Disturbance is the major threat to wildlife from visitors, both directly from people's activities and indirectly from tourist development. Species that live in towns, such as the house sparrow, adapt easily to the presence of people, but others can be driven away by humans. Black-necked cranes winter in the Phobjika valley in Bhutan; they are

Animals such as dolphins and chimpanzees are known to feed less and become more watchful when observed by tourists.

used to local people who wear traditional dress in muted colours and largely ignore the cranes. In contrast, tourists in brightly coloured clothing, who approach too close with cameras, frighten away the cranes.

Glowworms in Springbrook National Park, Australia, use their glow to attract insects on which to feed. If they are caught in torchlight beams used to guide tourists on special tours, they reduce the intensity of their glow and find fewer insects to eat.

Tourist hotels and restaurants adjacent to sea-turtle nesting beaches often disturb females attempting to lay eggs and hatchling turtles trying to reach the sea. Tourist development is blamed for the decline of green turtles breeding on the Maldives, for example.

Animals are at risk from disturbance by visitors during their breeding season. If separated from their mother, cubs of big cats like leopards may be killed by another predator. Eventually populations are threatened if breeding success is reduced.

Reducing Risks to Wildlife

There are many opportunities to reduce or avoid visitors disturbing wildlife. Visitor numbers can be limited and their movements controlled. Trained guides can accompany visitor groups. Walkways reduce damage to vegetation. Viewing hides can be provided. With good planning, visitor facilities can be situated well away from areas sensitive for wildlife. Instructing tourists on how to treat wildlife with respect has also proved effective.

The Serengeti National Park in Kenya has three zones for wildlife watching and other uses, as well as a zone where tourists are not allowed. Bunaken National Marine Park in Indonesia has a no-fishing zone, used for recreational diving and snorkelling. Having these zones avoids conflict between visitors and fishermen, and fish stocks have increased.

CASE STUDY

Australia: Penguin Parade

Phillip Island Nature Park is Australia's most popular natural wildlife attraction. In the nesting season up to 2,000 penguins come ashore each evening to their burrows in sand dunes on the beach. Visitors flock to watch the penguin parade. However, they are carefully controlled so they only view penguins in a relatively small area, leaving many other areas free from tourists. The penguin parade is mainly watched from fenced boardwalks or from a viewing tower. Rangers give information about the penguins, their ecology and behaviour. In 2005 as much as £2.9 million was raised in park admission fees and another £1.3 million from sales of souvenirs and refreshments. As well as funding tourist facilities, money from tourists supports research and conservation on the island.

Viewing of the penguin parade on Phillip Island in Australia is carefully managed to limit the impact on the surrounding environment.

Economic Benefits

Money from viewing wildlife comes from payments for entrance fees and permits to national parks and reserves, and from fees for guides and drivers. Visitors pay for accommodation and other services such as travel to wildlife-watching sites. Other parts of the economy also benefit, such as farmers who provide food for tourist restaurants and bakers who make bread for hotels. National governments gain revenue from tourist taxes and licence fees for hunting.

The value of an area for watching wildlife is often far higher than for an alternative use. Revenue generated by diving, snorkelling and coral viewing is around 10 to 20 times more than income from fishing in reef areas, for example. In the Maldives, divers spend £1.15 million a year on shark dives. This figure is estimated to be 100 times more than the export value of the shark meat. Income from tourism at turtle nesting sites is on average around three times higher than that from selling turtle meat or shells.

Wildlife watching such as scuba diving can be an important source of income for local communities.

A local guide stands by his safari vehicle in Tanzania. Here, programmes are in place to ensure that locals benefit from wildlife-watching activities.

Social Benefits

Funds raised from wildlife watching can be important in improving livelihoods of local people. In Kruger National Park in South Africa, payments from visitors exceed the cost of managing the park and support 3,000 local jobs. The Serena Hotels Group recently opened four luxury properties linked to game reserves in Tanzania, and employs 400 local people as full-time staff. Vegetables, fish and other foods are bought locally and so provide additional income for surrounding communities. Before developing the new properties, the group

CASE STUDY

Mexico: Monarch Butterflies

Every year, monarch butterflies migrate from their breeding grounds in North America to spend the winter in a few sites in the forests of Mexico. Although small, these areas can contain as many as 20 million butterflies. Two of the sites have been opened to tourists and huge numbers of visitors now enjoy the wonderful butterfly spectacle. A monarch butterfly project is working to protect forests and environmental resources throughout the region and to restore vital habitats for the butterflies. As well as successfully protecting the butterflies, the project has improved the livelihoods of the region's communities. Local people have been trained in tourism and employed as tourist guides, nature guards, in sales of arts and crafts and in construction work. Involving communities in all aspects of the project is helping to secure its long-term future.

Millions of monarch butterflies can spend the winter in just a few small sites in Mexico.

carried out studies to make sure that the impact on the local environment was minimised and that local communities would benefit as much as possible.

Leakage

Leakage means income from tourism that leaves the destination country. If tourism operators, hotels and restaurants replaced imported goods with local goods, more money would stay in the country. The tourist industry can also help by working with local producers to raise the quality of goods and services in order to meet tourist expectations. Tourists can make sure that payments they make for their holiday benefit their destination country as much as they can. Choosing a tour operator, airline and hotels owned by people from the country they are visiting are major steps. In Kenya, where safaris are a major attraction, steps are being taken to ensure that as much money as possible benefits local communities.

FACTS IN FOCUS
Leakage in LEDCs

The World Bank estimates that 55 per cent of income from international tourists leaves LEDCs through foreign-owned airlines, hotels and tour operators, or payments for imported food, drink and supplies. Studies in individual countries have put the figure even higher – 75 per cent in some Caribbean countries.

Conservation Benefits from Wildlife Watching

In many parts of the world, wildlife watching has become a powerful force for conservation. In Belize, for example, government taxes on tourists help support protected areas. On the Seychelles, visitor payments for organised boat trips to see whale sharks contribute to conservation. Whale sharks reach up to 18 m, and their huge size and rarity makes them a great attraction for divers and other tourists. The money raised helps to fund the Seychelles Marine Conservation Society research programme and to raise awareness of conserving these amazing animals.

Some tour operators donate a percentage of their profits to conservation projects. Since 1998, the UK tour operator Discovery Initiatives has donated over £25,000 a year to Tanjung Puting National Park in Kalimantan, Indonesia, through a partnership with the Orangutan Foundation. This money has been raised from just five tours a year.

Wildlife watching can encourage political and governmental support for species conservation. There is also an increasing number of schemes around the world targeted at young people – particularly students on a gap year between school and university – that involve monitoring wildlife for conservation.

Local Benefits

Wildlife watching can increase people's appreciation of the value of plants and animals in their national heritage. In Honduras, tourism partly funds schoolchildren from the capital on regular trips to La Tigra cloud forest visitor centre. Here they learn about the island's rainforest and its wildlife.

Money received from visitors can be a strong incentive for local communities and key stakeholders to conserve species and habitats that visitors have come to see. *Projeto Tamar* has helped to improve the numbers of sea turtles along the Brazilian coastline by protecting hatching turtles. This has been achieved by working with locals to create employment based on conserving turtles. The project has shown it is important for local people to receive a fair share of income if they stop collecting turtle eggs and instead try to protect them.

Tourists enjoy the coral reef off a beach in Hawaii. The tourism industry on the islands motivated the government to bring in new laws to protect the Hawaiian rainforest, native species and coral reefs.

CASE STUDY

Africa: Mountain Gorillas

Mountain gorillas are found in central Africa. They are endangered by the loss of their forest habitat and poaching. Gorillas are not fierce animals – they are shy, gentle and highly intelligent. They live in family groups, each led by a dominant male called a silverback. Several gorilla groups are now used to being visited by tourists and are not disturbed by them. Tourists pay as much as £175 a day to watch mountain gorillas, as well as paying park entrance fees and for their guides. Many conservationists believe that mountain gorillas would not have survived without the international attention they have received.

A recent survey showed an increase in population in gorilla groups that have become used to tourists or researchers.

The Galapagos Islands

The Galapagos Islands are probably the only place in the world where it is possible to experience what our planet was like before humans. Full of life, the islands attract visitors from all over the world. The 19 islands are very isolated, lying 1,000 km from the coast of Ecuador and at the meeting point of three ocean currents. The islands' unique location has led to the development of unusual animal life, such as the marine iguana, giant tortoise and many species of finch. In 1978 the Galapagos Islands became the first place in the world to be recognised as a World Heritage Site by the United Nations. In 2007, however, the World Heritage Committee put the islands on the its danger list.

Endangered species such as the giant Galapagos tortoise are under threat from rising visitor numbers.

EXPERT VIEW

'The Galapagos are in danger of being over-occupied by tourists and for a long time I have been worried about it. The number of visitors used to be under control and they could only land when conservationists were with them. Now there are so many tourists that they want to land a thousand people at a time and you simply cannot do that without destroying the islands.'

PROFESSOR RICHARD KEYNES, GREAT-GRANDSON OF CHARLES DARWIN

Problems for Wildlife and the Environment

Growth in tourism has promoted local businesses and the islands' population has doubled in the past 30 years. The rising traffic of people and goods has increased the number of non-native species in the area, especially rats, goats and pigs. These introduced species compete with native species for food. They also prey on the eggs and young of reptiles and birds. Human activity has caused pollution and habitat destruction in this once-untouched environment. Non-native plants now outnumber native plants. A quarter of all plant species and a half of bird, mammal and reptile species on the islands are believed to be endangered.

The increasing numbers of people have led to overfishing in the surrounding marine reserve. Harvesting of sharks for shark-fin soup and sea cucumbers for Chinese medicine is rising as international demand has grown.

A Sustainable Future for the Galapagos?

Adding the islands to the World Heritage danger list has highlighted the need for action to save the Galapagos. The high economic importance to Ecuador is also encouraging conservation efforts.

Strict limits on visitor numbers to the Galapagos and enforcing codes of behaviour would be major steps in providing a sustainable future for the islands.

Smartvoyager, a programme that certifies boats on the islands as meeting environmental standards, has been in place since 2001. This programme is voluntary, but if all visitors made sure they only used Smartvoyager boats, it would help to protect the islands. Visitors can also limit their impact on the environment by using the local companies working alongside conservationists. These local companies are making sure that growth is in the quality of services and not in quantity.

Raising environmental awareness among tourists and residents can also help, especially in inspiring local people to be proud of their islands and to protect them. Fisheries need to be managed effectively. Numbers of immigrant people could be restricted. Controlling introduced species is vital, although this is difficult. For instance, goats were successfully removed from one of the islands, but this was very expensive. Efforts are now underway to remove three introduced rat species on the islands.

Nature and Leisure Activities

Increasing numbers of people are spending their leisure time in natural environments. Walking, cycling and horse riding have been enjoyed for a long time, but new activities such as white-water rafting and sea kayaking are also becoming popular. These leisure activities, and the large numbers of people who enjoy them, affect wildlife areas at home and abroad.

Wear and Tear

All leisure activities can potentially harm the environment in some way. Wildlife in rivers can be disturbed by canoeists and white-water rafters, for example. Too many visitors in a limited area can damage habitats by trampling. This can be avoided by careful management. The Pennine Way is England's most popular long-distance path and has suffered severely from erosion – so much so that the erosion here can be seen from space. Paving the path for much of its length has

The Cumberland Plateau is one of North America's most outstanding areas of natural beauty.

prevented further erosion, and now vegetation has started to grow back.

In the United States, the Nature Conservancy has recently completed an agreement to begin a programme in the Cumberland Plateau, a large region of forests and mountains in Tennessee. The area is home to many unique species of animal and plants, and for years it remained an undeveloped wilderness. However, increased logging of the forests and larger visitor numbers began to degrade the area. The programme will provide a valuable wildlife corridor for birds and animals, and certain areas will be set aside for recreational activities such as hiking and fishing. By controlling logging and leisure activities in the Cumberland Plateau, the wear and tear on this precious environment can be limited and some of the damage reversed.

Wadi-Bashing

In the United Arab Emirates, dune- and wadi-bashing are among the most popular outdoor activities. A wadi is a dry river bed that only flows with water after rains and so is ideal for off-road driving. Quad bikes and four-wheel drive vehicles are used. People find wadi-bashing fun and exciting. It can provide a wonderful desert experience and challenging driving. However, unless carried out responsibly it can be extremely destructive to the environment. Tracks can easily be created that will last for decades, vegetation may be uprooted and desert wildlife disturbed. Damage by quad bikes and four-wheel drive vehicles can be limited if only existing tracks are used. In Namibia, guided trips by responsible operators are offered in dune areas that have been set aside for use by off-road vehicles. By restricting off-road vehicles in this way, the remaining dune areas can be protected successfully.

Quad bikers in Namibia, where special areas have been set aside for the activity, limiting the damage to the environment.

CASE STUDY

Australia: Walking in the Alps National Park

Mount Kosciuszko, the summit area of continental Australia's highest mountain, is a honeypot for tourists in the Australian Alps National Park. Around 70,000 people visit the alpine area during the snow-free period each year and about 21,000 of them take the day's walk to the summit and back. Environmental impacts include soil erosion, the introduction and spread of weeds, pollution of lakes and creeks, and loss of vegetation. In response, the park has hardened tracks, provided toilets, tried to educate visitors and restricted camping around the lakes in the park. These actions have helped to reduce the negative impact of tourism in the park.

Efforts have been made to educate visitors to Mount Kosciuszko about the damaging impacts of human activity in the region.

Wild Places in Urban Areas

There are a number of national parks close to population centres that offer opportunities for millions of people to enjoy wilderness in their leisure time. The Lake District, England's largest national park, lies close to one of the most densely populated parts of the UK and receives around 12 million visitors a year. In the eighteenth century the beauty of the landscape inspired William Wordsworth, one of England's most famous poets and amongst the first to write about the wonder of nature.

In Australia, the Royal National Park lies only 32 km from Sydney. The park packs incredible natural diversity into a small area. It is hugely popular with Sydney residents, who enjoy great surf beaches, clifftop walks, rainforest cycle tracks and riverside picnics in the park.

The Everglades National Park in Florida is the largest subtropical wilderness in the United States. It protects a fragile ecosystem of swamps and slow-moving rivers. The park attracts a million visitors a year. Activities include tram tours that take visitors through the wide range of park habitats, hiking, bird watching and kayaking.

As well as enjoying large wilderness areas, many people can enjoy nature in places that are close to home in their leisure time, such as a pond rich in aquatic life or walking in local woodland.

Artificial Landscapes and Habitats

Opportunities for recreation can also be found in habitats and landscapes that people have created, either by design or by accident. Often these have developed into rich places for wildlife.

Wreck diving has become one of the most fascinating and exciting experiences for recreational scuba divers. The wreck of the MV *Dania* near Mombasa in Kenya is a much-visited tourist dive site. It lies close to a coral reef and gradually corals, sponges and algae from the reef have settled here. Other marine life from the reef has colonised the wreck and it now acts as an extension to the reef. Diving in such an area can damage the marine life.

Creating artificial landscapes can be harmful to the environment. As growing numbers of people want to ski and snow is often not available, fake snow is increasingly being used to create ski runs. Making fake snow presents problems for the

Visitors can enjoy the scenery of the Florida Everglades from boats on the slow-moving rivers.

environment as vast amounts of water and energy are needed. Polluting chemicals are also used to ensure the formation of snow crystals. Is the harm this causes the environment justified when such places are created purely for human enjoyment?

In many cases wrecks have become valuable as homes and breeding grounds for marine life, as well as attracting divers.

CASE STUDY

Dubai: Ski Mountain

Ski Dubai in the United Arab Emirates has one of the world's largest indoor ski slopes, measuring 400 m long and using 6,000 tonnes of snow. Fake snow powder is available all year round and the temperature in the dome is kept at a degree or two below freezing. There is an 85 m high 'mountain', with five ski slopes that can be reached by chair and tow lifts. Another feature of Ski Dubai is the world's largest snow park, covering 3,000 sq m. Visitors can go tobogganing, take bobsled rides, enjoy the snowball-throwing gallery, make snowmen and experience regular snowfalls – in an area where outside temperatures can reach 40°C in the summer! Vast amounts of energy and water were needed to create the snow for the ski slopes and snow park, and will be required continually to maintain them.

Ski Dubai provides a ski resort in the middle of a scorching desert.

Skiing

Spectacular mountain scenery is a major attraction of winter skiing. It might seem as though winter skiing in natural surroundings is environmentally friendly and just leaves behind tracks in the snow, but it has long-lasting and damaging impacts.

Problems for the Environment

The ski industry has led to sharp increases in traffic, which causes noise and air pollution. There are now extended settlements of tourist buildings in many relatively remote areas that were once free from development. In the European Alps there are around 300 ski areas covering over 3,400 sq km. Up to 700,000 skiers use Switzerland's mountain slopes on any one day during the peak season.

Most downhill skiing takes place on slopes that have been made into suitable runs by the removal of trees, levelling of land and carving of pathways. Pylons, ski lifts and tows are erected.

Climate change means there is now less snow at lower altitudes so fake snow-making has increased. This has led to over-use of energy and water, and pollution by the chemicals used to help form the snow. Another outcome of climate change is that skiing is often limited to higher altitudes, which are more sensitive to environmental impacts. In addition, litter does not break down easily in mountain environments. Wildlife may be disturbed by skiers and ski developments.

Ski lifts, cable cars and other constructions all spoil the mountain scenery.

Sustainable Solutions

There is great potential for the skiing industry to become more energy efficient. For example, in the United States, 61 ski resorts in 18 states use renewable energy – mainly wind. This has many uses, including powering ski lifts.

Ski resorts can show their commitment to a sustainable future for the industry as a whole by signing up to 'Sustainable Slopes – the Environmental Charter for Ski Areas'. Ski holiday agents and tourists planning skiing holidays can make sure their destination has signed up to the charter. Skiers can take action to make skiing more sustainable by:
- Planning to travel to the ski resort by train or bus rather than by air and/or car.
- Considering cross-country skiing or snow-shoeing, as these forms of skiing do not require graded slopes and ski lifts.
- Conserving energy at lodges by turning off lights when leaving the room and keeping heating to a minimum.
- Reducing and recycling any waste produced.
- Disposing of waste properly and never throwing anything from a ski lift.
- Reducing disturbance to wildlife by being quiet and listening to the sounds of nature.

FACTS IN FOCUS
National Ski Areas Association Sustainable Slopes Charter

The Sustainable Slopes Charter is a set of voluntary guidelines written by the National Ski Area Association. The guidelines include cutting down on waste, saving energy and water, and forest and wildlife management programmes. More than 330 ski resorts in North America, as well as ski resorts in Europe, have signed the charter. A 2004 study accused some ski areas participating in the Sustainable Slopes initiative of greenwashing. The study provided evidence that these ski areas were only putting up a front of environmental concern while ignoring the larger problems created by the skiing industry. Despite this criticism the charter has created awareness of the need to be environmentally responsible, and substantial cuts in energy and water use have resulted from the initiative.

Physical Impacts of Human Activity

Physical impacts, such as land clearing and construction work to develop areas for visitors, have often damaged the environment. Ongoing human encroachment into wild areas can also cause harm – for example, the wash from fast-moving speedboats can erode river banks. Some ecosystems are particularly fragile, including alpine regions, rainforests, wetlands and coral reefs. These ecosystems are often at risk because they are very attractive to both visitors and developers.

Tourism Development

Poorly planned tourism development, such as accommodation, restaurants and recreation facilities, can destroy wildlife habitats and spoil attractive landscapes. Development may involve sand mining and cause sand-dune erosion. Tourist buildings may clash with local architecture or look out of place in a natural environment. Better land-use planning can overcome these problems, however. In some new resorts care is being taken to use local materials and to build in the style of traditional architecture.

Coastal wetlands have often been drained and filled in to create sites for tourism development, such as in Jamaica. In many tropical countries, coastal saltwater forests called mangroves form vital coastal protection. The mangroves are also valuable to local communities as a source of food, fuel and building materials. Large areas of mangroves have now been cleared to make way for resorts in places like the Philippines, leaving coasts at risk from erosion.

The environment of many resorts in the Mediterranean, the world's leading tourist destination, has been seriously damaged by poorly managed resort development.

Marinas can severely damage the fragile marine ecosystem in coastal areas.

Mining and Marina Construction

In the Maldive islands, coral was once mined and widely used in building tourist developments. Current regulations discourage this, but coral is still being mined in the Maldives and used to build breakwaters and jetties. As the coral reefs are important breeding grounds for fish, local people have suffered as the number of fisheries has reduced.

Without careful planning, marina construction can harm coastal environments by causing changes in currents and coastlines. A new marina proposed for Baja in the Los Cabos estuary in Mexico is the most ambitious development project in the area for a generation. There will be up to 500 boats, as well as hotels and beach clubs, but conservationists point out that the marina seriously threatens wildlife and the environment.

Road Building

Unless well-designed, road construction can cause habitat loss and spoil landscapes. An example of this is in the European Alps, the world's most-visited mountains. People go there to enjoy the beautiful mountain scenery, but in some places the views are ruined by a network of roads, and wildlife has been driven away.

EXPERT VIEW

'Local people are the most valuable resource for protecting biodiversity and landscapes. If there are thriving communities on Lastovo [an island off Croatia] that benefit from nature, then protection will be sustainable. But it won't be if the communities die. This is extremely important – it's not just the island's nature that needs to be saved, but also its people.'
REPRESENTATIVE FROM A NON-GOVERNMENTAL ORGANISATION IN CROATIA

CASE STUDY

Algiers: Sidi-Fredj Resort

Algiers has great potential for attracting visitors. Its beaches are among the best in Africa. Tourism development is only just beginning in Algiers and a new resort, Sidi-Fredj, has been constructed. Planning regulations were carefully followed so the resort was sustainable. The complex includes four hotels, an activity centre, open-air theatre, and leisure and green spaces. There is also a marina with a yacht harbour. The architecture of the resort is based on the traditional Algerian style. Local building materials have been used wherever possible. Efficient water and energy use are included in the design.

Plastic bags and other waste spoil the scenery on a beach in Greece.

Pollution

Human activity can cause widespread pollution in the world's wild places. Air pollutants, litter and other solid waste, sewage, chemicals, oil and noise may all be produced. However, there are many ways for organisations and individuals to limit the damage.

FACTS IN FOCUS
Sewage

Waste water from hotels can cause serious pollution of coastal waters and lakes close to visitor attractions, putting the health of people and wildlife at risk. Coral reefs are especially threatened. The nutrients in sewage encourage the growth of algae, which smother and eventually kill the corals.

Solid Waste and Litter

Waste disposal can often be a pressing issue where there are high numbers of visitors. If not disposed of properly, litter can spoil the natural environments that attracted people in the first place. Plastic bags are one of the worst litter problems as they are unsightly, usually do not decompose easily and are a danger to wildlife. Large numbers of marine animals die after eating plastic bags. Sea turtles mistake clear plastic for the jellyfish that they eat and so often swallow the bags.

Many countries are taking action to get rid of plastic bags. In countries such as Australia, Germany and Ireland, shoppers must now buy plastic bags rather than being given them free of charge. Some supermarkets in the United Kingdom have also adopted this policy. In June 2008 shops in China were banned from giving out free plastic bags. Coles Bay in Tasmania, Australia,

CASE STUDY

Caribbean: The Mesoamerican Reef

The Mesoamerican Reef in the Caribbean is the world's second-largest barrier reef. It is also one of the most endangered by coastal development and pollution. In 2004 the non-profit group Conservation International began a programme called the Mesoamerican Reef Tourism Initiative. The programme works with local governments, hoteliers, developers, cruise lines and local dive and water-sports associations in Mexico, Belize and Honduras. Cruise lines have now agreed that any waste water from their ships is discharged at least 6.4 km from any marine ecosystems. Efforts are being made to limit snorkelling by visitors to just one section of the reef, leaving the rest undisturbed. The Reef Initiative is also helping coastal hotels in southern Belize and on the Riviera Maya in Mexico to conserve energy and water, and to reduce solid waste and the use of chemicals.

became the nation's first plastic bag-free town in 2003. Plastic bags were banned from the entire country of Bhutan as long ago as 1998.

Mountaineers and tourists often leave a large amount of litter in mountain areas. For instance, on Mount Kenya a group of four mountain climbers can produce on average 20 kg of rubbish within just four days. Since 1993, students of the Mountain Climbing Club of Kenya have taken the lead in an annual clean-up on the mountain. The tour operator Gecko Adventures organises annual 'Clean up the Nile' trips at a subsided cost, clearing rubbish from campsites on the River Nile in Egypt.

Cruise Ships

The amount of polluting waste from cruise ships can be enormous. A week-long voyage on a cruise ship with 3,000 passengers and workers produces an average of 954 litres of sewage, 590 litres of hazardous waste and eight tonnes of solid waste. In the Caribbean, more than three-quarters of all waste from ships comes from cruise ships. Some cruise lines are now working to reduce waste. One cruise company has started a zero-discharge policy, meaning that its waste water has no pollutants. Some new ships now have built-in waste-management systems.

Cruise tourists can help by asking questions about practices such as waste disposal on board.

Road Traffic

Visitor cars, buses and planes create noise in areas that were once quiet. The noise often disrupts the peaceful atmosphere that people have come to enjoy. Natural sounds such as birdsong and running water can no longer be heard properly. Animals are often disturbed and even frightened away.

Road traffic is high in the European Alps, especially around tourist resorts and on scenic minor roads. Polluting vehicle emissions have risen, causing damage to forests through acid rain.

Each weekend at the busy St Gotthard Pass in Switzerland, traffic releases 30 tonnes of nitrogen oxides, for example. The effects of air pollution are more serious at high altitudes, where the air is thinner. Careful management can successfully reduce the impact of road traffic. In the 1990s in Triglav National Park, Slovenia, in the south-eastern Alps, the increasing number of visitors was causing traffic problems and disturbance. Access by car is now controlled on roads in the park, speed restrictions have been introduced and car parking is regulated.

Restrictions on traffic in the Triglav National Park in Slovenia have helped preserve the natural beauty of the area, and have limited noise and air pollution.

CASE STUDY

United States: Yosemite National Park

Yosemite National Park sees 3.5 million visitors each year. Vehicle traffic has risen by about 30 per cent over the last 10 years and the numbers of roads and car parks have increased to keep pace. This has led to habitat loss in the park and deaths of bears and other animals hit by vehicles. Smog caused by car emissions is harming plants and animals, and is sometimes so thick that the park cannot be seen from the air. Major steps are now being taken taken to encourage visitors to avoid using their cars and reduce pressure on Yosemite. Free shuttle-bus services run throughout the park. Some buses cater especially for hikers visiting popular spots. During the ski season a free bus travels between Yosemite valley and the ski area. Some car parks have even been removed.

Cars rumble through the beautiful scenery in Yosemite National Park in the United States. The sheer volume of traffic resulted in initiatives to limit vehicles in the park.

National Park Traffic Schemes

In several national parks, including the New Forest and Peak District in England, large volumes of visitor traffic are causing high levels of noise and air pollution. This can irritate residents and the visitors themselves. Popular attractions in the parks are increasingly overcrowded at weekends and at holiday times. In the Goyt Valley, a much-visited area in the Peak District, traffic was even more of a problem because the approach roads were too narrow for coaches. This was overcome by introducing a successful scheme in which the central part of the valley was closed to traffic at peak times. Car parks have been created and visitors are encouraged to enjoy the valley on foot.

The Goyt Valley, in the United Kingdom's Peak District.

Polar regions – some of the wildest, most untouched places in the world – will be dramatically affected by climate change.

Climate Change

Climate change is widely considered to be the world's greatest environmental threat, affecting both LEDCs and MEDCs. The contribution of air travel to climate change is perhaps one of the most pressing environmental problems caused by human activity.

Carbon dioxide released into the atmosphere is the major cause of climate change, and air travel is the fastest-growing source. Although flights only contribute about 3.5 per cent of carbon-dioxide emissions, this could rise to 15 per cent by 2050 if no measures are taken. Global tourism is closely linked to climate change because tourism is responsible for 60 per cent of air travel. If climate change continues as it is now, or as climate scientists predict, then many holiday destinations will change forever. Tropical rainforests, many coastal resorts, Arctic and Antarctic regions, and alpine ski resorts are among those most likely to be affected. For this reason many people think that no holidays abroad can be sustainable if travel is by plane. Does this mean people should stop flying when going on holiday, to save the environment?

If air travel stopped, many LEDCs would become much poorer, as international tourism is important to their economies. They depend on foreign tourists as the main income source or as a major boost to their earnings. Almost all these countries can only be reached for a holiday visit by air. So is there a way of flying more sustainably?

Carbon Offsetting

Some travel companies encourage tourists to take part in carbon offsetting. Offsetting means paying an extra small cost for a holiday. The company uses this money to organise projects such as tree-planting, often in the country of destination. The trees absorb the same amount of carbon dioxide as emitted during the flight. There is some debate

TAKE ACTION

You can help cut carbon emissions when going on holiday by:
- Taking a holiday in your home country rather than travelling abroad.
- Using environmentally friendly transport – buses or trains instead of cars and planes – when travelling about on holiday. Travelling the same distance by train produces a third of the carbon emissions of air travel.
- Choosing no more than one long-haul flight a year and perhaps having a longer stay.
- Avoiding flying abroad for a short break.

These trees have been planted as part of a carbon-offsetting scheme.

about whether carbon offsetting is effective, though. There is no guarantee that a new forest will be permanent. The forest may be cut or burnt down, or the trees may die from disease and then carbon dioxide will be released again. Tree plantations, especially of introduced species, often damage the environment by consuming large amounts of water, for instance. A better solution may be to research alternative fuels, such as biofuels, or to find more efficient engine designs for aircraft.

Inbound Tourism by Means of Transport (2006)

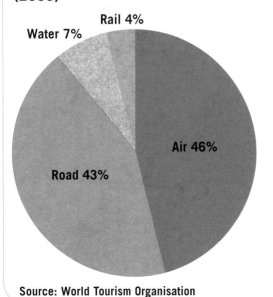

- Rail 4%
- Water 7%
- Air 46%
- Road 43%

Source: World Tourism Organisation

FACTS IN FOCUS
Eurostar Environmental Action Plan

Eurostar is the high-speed passenger rail service that runs between the United Kingdom and mainland Europe. In 2007 plans were announced to make high-speed rail a greener option for travel in northern Europe. Eurostar plans to reduce its emissions and minimise the impact on the environment of all its operations. Energy meters have been installed to make sure the trains are driven as economically as possible. Eurostar's aims are to be as energy efficient as possible. They plan to cut consumption of raw materials and make recycling of waste a priority.

Eurostar has a target of reducing carbon-dioxide emissions by 25 per cent for each traveller journey by 2012.

Natural Resources

Human activities in wild places put a lot of pressure on natural resources. This can cause problems for local communities, especially those in LEDCs where resources can often be scarce and precious. Both renewable and non-renewable natural resources are affected, including soil, wetlands, minerals, forests and wildlife.

Water Resources

The tourism industry frequently overuses water for hotels and hotel grounds, swimming pools and golf courses. Tourists can make the situation worse by using more water on holiday than they do when at home. In general tourists use far more water than a local person. A study in the Philippines found that a hotel guest uses as much water in 18 days as a rural family does in a year.

Despite this record of high consumption, there are great opportunities for water savings in the tourist industry. Hilton Hotels and Marriott International, two major international hotel chains, are investigating ways of reducing water use, and others are already putting plans into action. New hotels can include water-use efficiency in the planning stages. Existing hotels can make environmental checks of current water use and then make action plans to become more efficient. LeSport Resort on St Lucia saved 454,545 litres in a year by recycling 'greywater' (run-off from washing). By reducing the volume of water each time a toilet is flushed, Hotel Beausejour in New Brunswick, Canada, saved 120,000 litres of water a year.

High water consumption for tourism can lead to a serious reduction of water supplies that locals and the tourism industry depend on.

Solar panels on the roof of a hotel in Greece help reduce energy use from fossil fuels.

FACTS IN FOCUS
Golf Courses

Worldwide, 50 million people play golf on 25,000 golf courses, and the sport continues to increase in popularity. Golf courses require huge amounts of water. A Philippines study found that the average golf course uses enough water to irrigate 65 hectares of farmland in the country per year. In Thailand a typical golf course uses as much water as 60,000 rural villagers. Even in Spain, a golf course in Benidorm uses as much water as 10,000 people.

EXPERT VIEW

'The beaches of Goa in south India were reported to be very clean with dense vegetation and magnificent dunes three decades ago. Overuse of the beaches for tourism-related activities has severely damaged the sand-dune habitats.'
INDIAN SCIENTIST RESEARCHERS

Energy Use

Energy use by tourists is often very high. Saving energy can reduce costs considerably, often in a very short time, and also cut emissions of carbon dioxide, helping to limit climate change. Hotels can be especially wasteful of energy, but there are great opportunities to make savings. These can be achieved by becoming more energy efficient or by switching to renewable energy sources, such as solar power. One example is the Taj Hotel chain in India, which uses solar heating to supply between 50 and 100 per cent of hot water in its hotels. The group found that the initial investment paid for itself in as little as two years.

Recycling

There is great potential to reduce waste and save money at the same time in the tourism industry. Monte Carlo Hotel in Las Vegas built recycling facilities into the hotel design. This saves £14,000 – 15,000 a year on waste-hauling costs. Banff Springs Hotel in Canada cut waste by more than 85 per cent through its recycling programme. By placing recycling bins in 70 rooms, Toronto's Skydome Hotel collects 58,000 cans and 12,000 bottles a year.

Large amounts of waste food are thrown out each day, and this has led some hotels to use their own composters. Mount Nelson is South Africa's oldest and grandest hotel. It has a wormery with over a million worms that break down the hotel's food waste to compost, which fertilises the hotel's 36,400 sq m of gardens.

Logging activity has caused orangutans to become endangered, by destroying their habitat in places such as Sumatra and Borneo.

Nature for Nature's Sake

While conserving nature for human enjoyment is helping to preserve some important natural areas around the world, it is important to remember that these places should also be preserved for their own sake and for the resources they sustain. Logging in forests the world over, mining in mountain regions, drilling for oil in ocean environments – all are necessary activities to gain resources, but they must be managed in a sustainable way to ensure these resources last. They should also be carried out in ways that limit the effects on wildlife. Alternative resources could be used to preserve dwindling fossil fuels.

World Wildlife

Our planet operates on a fragile natural balance, and preserving ecosystems such as rainforests and marine environments is crucial to the long-term survival of many species of plants and animals. Although preservation efforts around the world are limiting damage in this area, thousands of species are already extinct or endangered because of human activity. In the past two centuries deforestation has slowly contributed to climate change, as trees play an important part in maintaining the balance of greenhouse gases in the atmosphere. There will become a 'tipping point', a time when the damage done by humans to the natural world can no longer be reversed. That time is not far in the future, so everyone should play a part in ensuring that the world's wild places are respected and preserved – for future generations to enjoy, and for the future of our planet as a whole.

CASE STUDY

Canada: The Great Bear Rainforest

The Great Bear Rainforest is a large area of temperate rainforest in Canada. It makes up a quarter of all that is left of this type of forest worldwide. It is the habitat for thousands of species of plants and animals, many of which are under threat. In 2007, the Canadian government announced plans to support a conservation programme introduced by a coalition of several environmental groups that would establish a series of protected areas in the rainforest. More than two million hectares of rainforest will be protected from logging activities, safeguarding habitats for the plants and animals that live there.

A grizzly bear in the Great Bear Rainforest in Canada, an area now subject to a huge preservation programme.

Facts and Figures

International Tourist Arrivals (1990–2006)

Year	No. of tourist arrivals
1990	436,000,000
1995	536,000,000
2000	684,000,000
2005	803,000,000
2006	846,000,000

Top 10 Countries by Tourist Arrivals (2006)

Country	No. of tourist arrivals
France	79,100,000
Spain	58,500,000
United States	51,100,000
China	49,600,000
Italy	41,100,000
United Kingdom	30,700,000
Germany	23,600,000
Mexico	21,400,000
Austria	20,300,000
Russia	20,200,000

International Tourism Income (1990–2006)

Year	Income (US$ billion)
1990	264
1995	405
2000	474
2005	676
2006	733

International Tourism

- International tourist arrivals totalled 846 million in 2006.
- On average the growth in international tourist arrivals was 6.5 per cent a year between 1950 and 2006.
- In 2020, international tourist arrivals worldwide are predicted to be 1.6 billion.

Sustainable Tourism

- In Europe 20–30 per cent of travellers are aware of the needs and values of sustainable tourism.
- In Germany, environmental quality is expected by 65 per cent of travellers and over 40 per cent think it is particularly important to find environmentally friendly accommodation.
- In a recent survey, as many as 87 per cent of UK tourists said their holiday should not damage the environment.
- More than two thirds of US and Australian travellers and 90 per cent of British tourists believe active protection of the environment and support of local communities should be part of the responsibility of hotel management.

further Resources

Websites

http://www.conservation.org/
Conservation International – a US-based conservation organisation that works internationally.

http://www.wilderness.org/
The Wilderness Society (USA) – protects wilderness and inspires Americans to care for their wild places.

http://www.wilderness.org.au/
The Wilderness Society (Australia) – defends wilderness areas across Australia.

http://www.world-tourism.org/
World Tourism Organisation – up-to-date statistics and information on tourism.

http://www.responsibletravel.com/
Responsible Travel – lots of background information and advice on having a responsible holiday.

http://www.unep.fr/greenpassport/
Green Passport – information on how to have a sustainable holiday.

http://www.panda.org
WWF International – an international organisation working to conserve the Earth's wildlife and environments.

http://www.lonelyplanet.com/responsibletravel/
Lonely Planet Responsible Tourism

Books

Dove, Jane, *Tourism and Recreation* (Access to Geography), Hodder & Stoughton, 2004

Griffin, Tony and Peter Williams (eds.), *Sustainable Tourism*, Butterworth Heinemann, 2002

Inskipp, Carol, *Healthy Seas* (Sustainable Futures), Evans Publishing, 2005

Inskipp, Carol, *Travel and Tourism* (The Global Village), Evans Publishing, 2008

Lorimer, Kerry, *Code Green: Experiences of a Lifetime*, Lonely Planet, 2006

Mabey, Richard, *Nature Cure*, Chatto and Windus, 2006

Macfarlane, Robert, *The Wild Places*, Granta Books, 2007

Mittermeier, Russ, *Wilderness*, Conservation International, 2003

Glossary

biodiversity all the plants, animals, insects and fungi in a particular region.

certification a process in which an official body such as a government or organisation ensures that an area or industry meets particular standards.

climate change a change in global temperatures that can result in extreme weather conditions. Climate change can happen naturally, but human activities are increasing the rate of this change.

composter a container in which organic matter (such as food waste or dead leaves) is allowed to decay to make compost, which is often then used as a fertiliser.

conservation the active management of the Earth's natural resources and the environment to ensure their quality is maintained and that they are wisely used.

conservationist a person who looks after the environment.

coral reef an underwater ecosystem formed from large numbers of tiny animals with hard skeletons. Coral reefs are some of the most productive and spectacular ecosystems in the world.

ecology the study of how living things interact with one another and their environment.

economy the supply of money gained by a community or country from goods and services.

ecosystem all the plants and animals in an area, along with their environment.

erosion the wearing away of rock or soil by natural processes such as wind or water, or by human activity such as farming.

exploitation the use of natural resources in a way that harms the environment or local people.

fossil fuels energy sources that have been created over millions of years by the decay of once-living organisms. Coal, oil and natural gas are examples of fossil fuels.

greenwashing when tourism companies mislead tourists into thinking their holidays are environmentally friendly when they are not.

gross domestic product (GDP) the value of all goods and services produced within a country in a given year.

habitat a place where a plant or animal lives.

indigenous naturally found in a country rather than coming from another place. The term can apply to people, plants or animals.

introduced species a species of plant or animal that does not occur naturally in an area, but which has been introduced from elsewhere.

LEDC less economically developed country – one of the poorer countries of the world. LEDCs include all of Africa, Asia (except Japan), Latin America and the Caribbean, and Melanesia, Micronesia and Polynesia.

livelihood a way of obtaining things that are needed for life, such as food and shelter.

mass tourism tourism on a large scale.

MEDC more economically developed country – one of the richer countries of the world. MEDCs include all of Europe, North America, Australia, New Zealand and Japan.

native species a species of plant or animal that occurs naturally in an area.

non-profit group a group or organisation whose activities do not make money.

nutrient a food or chemical needed by plants or animals for them to grow and thrive.

organic farming a system of farming that does not use chemical pesticides or artificial fertilisers.

pesticide a substance that kills pests, usually used by farmers to stop crops being eaten.

pollution harmful substances in the environment, often present as a result of human activity.

predator an animal that hunts or kills other animals for food.

protected area an area set aside to protect wildlife and its habitats.

rainforest forest that grows in an area that is very hot and that has high rainfall all year. Rainforests can support more types of plants and animals than any other ecosystem.

recycling the process by which materials are collected and used again as 'raw' materials for new products.

renewable energy energy generated from sources that can be replaced or renewed, such as the wind or the sun.

resource a stock or supply of materials or other useful or valuable things.

rural relating to the countryside.

smog a mixture of fog and smoke, forming an air pollutant.

species a particular type of animal or other living thing.

stakeholder an organisation or individual that has a stake or interest in the outcome of a particular project.

sustainability the use of natural resources in a way that means the present generation can have what it needs without damaging the supply for future generations.

tourism receipts money received from tourism.

United Nations an international organisation, established in 1945, which aims to help countries cooperate in matters of international law and economic and social development.

urban relating to built-up areas such as towns and cities.

wetlands areas that are made up of marshes or swamps, where water does not drain away naturally.

wilderness area land that has been unaffected by human activity.

World Heritage Site a place considered to be of outstanding cultural and natural importance. International operations help to conserve these areas.

Index